YOUR KNOWLEDGE HAS VALUE

AF136166

- We will publish your bachelor's and
  master's thesis, essays and papers

- Your own eBook and book -
  sold worldwide in all relevant shops

- Earn money with each sale

Upload your text at www.GRIN.com
and publish for free

Peer-To-Peer File Sharing. Music and Copyright in the Internet Age

Sebastian Just

Bibliographic information published by the German National Library:

The German National Library lists this publication in the National Bibliography; detailed bibliographic data are available on the Internet at http://dnb.dnb.de.

ISBN: 9783346813794
This book is also available as an ebook.

© GRIN Publishing GmbH
Nymphenburger Straße 86
80636 München

Print and binding: Books on Demand GmbH, Norderstedt, Germany
Printed on acid-free paper from responsible sources.

The present work has been carefully prepared. Nevertheless, authors and publishers do not incur liability for the correctness of information, notes, links and advice as well as any printing errors.

GRIN web shop: https://www.grin.com/document/1323708

Humboldt-Universität zu Berlin

Institut für Musikwissenschaft und Medienwissenschaft

Modul 5: Digitale Medien (SO 2019)

A material history of intellectual property and the public domain

Sommer 2020

Peer-to-peer file sharing: the digital demise of intellectual property?

Music and copyright in the internet age.

Sebastian Just

Bachelorkombinationsstudiengang Medienwissenschaften

4. Semester

Contents

1. Introduction   2

2. The loss of scarcity   4

3. Napster: the P2P-pioneer   8

   3.1 Motivation   8

   3.2 Structure   10

   3.3 Shutdown   12

4. P2P through the 2000s   13

   4.1 Decentralization   14

   4.2 Legal war   16

   4.3 Aftermath   17

5. The new music industry   19

6. Conclusion   20

List of references   22

1. Introduction

On the 3rd of April 1993, the World Wide Web (WWW) was made available to the public by the English computer scientist Tim Berners-Lee, who is often referred to as the inventor of the internet.[1] By connecting people all over the world, this technological milestone initiated drastic changes to how we are able to consume visual and acoustical entertainment. In 1999, the first ever file sharing network called Napster launched and illicitly enabled users to exchange copyrighted music for free.[2] This was accomplished by using a peer-to-peer (P2P) system, which takes advantage of the vast availability of the internet and the resultant high number of "peers". Users register to the network and declare which files from their computer they are willing to share, enabling others to download the files directly from them rather than through a central sever.[3] This sort of file transfer posed a challenge for the music industry, as their music was made publicly available with no one paying for it. In addition, P2P systems conflicted with the idea of intellectual property, which grants an author certain rights over his or her work in form of a copyright.

Since the emergence of audio tapes in the late 1960s, copyright law has been an important ally in the music industry's fight against the unauthorized duplication of music (generally referred to as "music piracy").[4] While the history of copyright goes way back to the the invention of the printing press in the 15th century, the first real copyright law, the Statute of Anne, was passed in 1710 in Great Britain and literally gave the author the "right to copy" – it was followed by the Copyright Act of 1790 in the United States.[5] The 1886 Berne Convention was the first international agreement concerning copyright law and together with it's revision in Berlin in 1908 it still acts as the foundation for to-

---

[1] Cf. Gil Press: "A Very Short History Of The Internet And The Web", in: *Forbes*, 02.01.2015, https://www.forbes.com/sites/gilpress/2015/01/02/a-very-short-history-of-the-internet-and-the-web-2/#7b71b77a7a4e, accessed 01.10.2020.

[2] Cf. Jim Rogers: *The death and the life of the music industry in the digital age*, London: Bloomsbury 2013, 58.

[3] Cf. Lu Liu/Nick Antonopoulos: "From Client-Server to P2P Networking", in: Xuemin Shen/Heather Yu/John Buford/Mursalin Akon (eds.): *Handbook of Peer-to-Peer Networking*, Berlin et al.: Springer 2009, 71-89, 75.

[4] Cf. Berit Kann: *Musikpiraterie: Ansätze zur Lösung der praktischen und juristischen Probleme unter besonderer Berücksichtigung des Urheberstrafrechts*, Münster: Lit 1995, 39.

[5] Cf. Jessica Litman: *Digital Copyright*, Amherst/New York: Prometheus Books 2001, 15.

days legislation.[6] Since they disagreed with requirements like the cross-border recognition of copyrighted works, the US remained outside the Berne Convention.[7] In 1952, they joined the Universal Copyright Convention (UCC), which functioned as an alternative to the Berne Convention for states that refused certain guidelines but still wanted to take part.[8] After more than 100 years the US eventually joined the Berne Convention in 1989 due to pressure from Hollywood.[9]

To establish the international agreements from the Berne Convention and the UCC on a national basis, the US passed the Copyright Act of 1976. The nation's copyright laws may differ in some aspects, but the most important guidelines are the same: An author's work is automatically protected by a copyright (no registration is needed) but only when it exists in a fixed form, which means that for example a whistled melody is not protected until it is recorded. The work must offer a distinct character and the author must have put some sort of manual effort as well as time into it. If the criteria are fulfilled, the author has the exclusive right to publish, copy, spread and publicly perform his work – he is also able to transfer these rights to people or companies.[10] The minimum term of protection as stated in the Berne Convention is the authors lifetime plus 50 years, with the US and EU extending it to 70 years after the authors death.[11] Due to the 1994 Agreement on Trade-Related Aspects of Intellectual Property Rights (TRIPS), all members of the World Trade Organization (WTO) who want to participate in trade have to adapt the standards of the Berne Convention.[12]

The first traces of P2P go back to the beginnings of the internet, which was originally laid out as a P2P system in which every user is an equal participant. In 1969, the so called ARPANET used P2P to share computing resources between the UCLA, Stanford

---

[6] Cf. Martin Kretschmer/Friedemann Kawohl: "The History and Philosophy of Copyright", in Simon Frith/Lee Marshall (eds.): *Music and Copyright*, Second edition, Edinburgh: Edinburgh University Press 2004, 21-53, 40.

[7] Cf. Matthew David: *Peer to Peer and the Music Industry: The Criminalization of Sharing*, Thousand Oaks: SAGE Publications 2010, 52.

[8] Cf. Joseph S. Dubin: "The Universal Copyright Convention", in: *California Law Review*, vol. 42, no. 1 (1954), 89-119, 89, https://www.jstor.org/stable/pdf/3478227.pdf?refreqid=excelsior%3A2a830f3fba-b813884261efb623f13405, accessed 02.10.2020.

[9] Cf. Martin Kretschmer/Friedemann Kawohl 2004, 40.

[10] On copyright criteria and rights: Cf. Martin Kretschmer: "Eine Lobby-Geschichte: Reflexionen zur Entwicklung des Urheberrechts", in: Lina Brion/Detlef Diederichsen (publ.): *100 Jahre Copyright*, Berlin: Matthes & Seitz, 74-99, 90-91.

[11] Cf. Martin Kretschmer/Friedemann Kawohl 2004, 40.

[12] Cf. Martin Kretschmer/Friedemann Kawohl 2004, 40.

Research Institute, UC Santa Barbara and the University of Utah. 10 years later it was established in the Usenet, which was developed by students from the University of North Carolina and Duke University to exchange files and messages through an operation system called Unix.[13]

The objective of this paper is to take a closer look at the development and behavior of P2P based file sharing networks while especially considering intellectual property law to assess the impact this disruptive technology had on the music industry.[14] To do that I will first look at the shift from analogue to digital audio, which entailed significant changes for both the music industry and the consumer. Then I will focus on the first real P2P file sharing network Napster, especially on why it came into being, how it worked and to what extend it interfered with copyright law. Afterwards I will look at the period after Napster's shutdown in 2001, in which various new P2P networks even more copyright-resistant emerged. I will examine how these networks functioned compared to their predecessor, how the music industry and the state tried to take on these "digital enemies" and how P2P affected the music business. Eventually I will look at how the industry managed to adapt to the internet, treating it as a profitable platform rather than a dystopian technology.

2. The loss of scarcity

"The major industry has always controlled the means of distribution up until the digital era, and that control has been lost."[15]

The most profitable branch of the music industry is made up by the volume and value of total record sales and had a worldwide revenue of $US37 billion in 2000. In the same year, this business was dominated by five big international companies, which controlled 80% of the global market: EMI, BMG, The Warner Music Group, Sony Music Entertainment and Universal/PolyGram. Sales leader was the US with a value of US$14 bil-

---

[13] Whole paragraph: Cf. Nelson Minar/Marc Hedlund: "A Network of Peers: Peer-to-Peer Models Through the History of the Internet", in: Andy Oram (ed.): *Peer-to-peer: Harnessing the benefits of a disruptive technology*, Sebastopol: O'Reilly 2001, 3-20, 4-6.

[14] I will focus on the US when looking at legal questions, since the European copyright law only differs to a small extend. Most P2P networks which are/were available in the US are/were also available in the EU and vice verca. Also, the important court cases took place in the US.

[15] Quote by Alison Wenham, chair of the AIM: Jim Rogers 2013, 29.

lion, followed by Europe (US$11 billion) and Japan (US$6.5 billion).[16] Being responsible for huge revenue losses, piracy has been an ongoing problem for the major music companies. In the 1990s, non-legitimate sales stood at 27 million units per year, which amounts up to US$280 million annually.[17] In Germany, piracy sales added up to 222 million DM in 1993.[18] In 2000, global piracy sale revenues were US$1.8 billion with most of the infringers coming from China, Russia and Mexico.[19]

With the release of the Compact Disc (CD) in 1982, consumers were able to purchase an album and to listen it – but nothin more, as the CD was in read-only format. Although there was technology available to copy this and other mediums, it was not user friendly and the quality worsened with every play. For a long time, quality music was only available through the commercial way. With the introduction of the Compact Disc Recordable (CD-R) in the 1990s, consumers were now able to copy music at home using a burner.[20] However, the major companies were not afraid of individual consumers home taping discs, as they would afterwards go purchase the music they like and in that way encourage more legal sales.[21] The whole perennial shift from vinyl to CD was very profitable for the music companies since old collections could be reformatted and sold again.[22] A lot of people wanted to replace their vinyl collection with CDs and were therefore fine with paying a higher price for the new technology.[23] One of the first people to express concern towards the new CD-R format was the chairman of CBS Records UK and the British Phonographic Industry, Maurice Oberstein: "Do you realise we are giving away our master tapes here?"[24] He was aware of the fact that the loss of scarcity could endanger the major company's monopoly while at the same time lowering the consumer's esteem towards music.

---

[16] Revenue data until here: Cf. David Throsby: *The music industry in the new millennium: Global and local perspectives*, Paris: UNESCO Division of Arts and Cultural Enterprise 2002, 3-4.

[17] Cf. David Throsby 2002, 11.

[18] Cf. Berit Kann 1995, 46.

[19] Cf. David Throsby 2002, 11.

[20] Paragraph until here: Cf. Lee Marshall: "Infringers", in Simon Frith/Lee Marshall (eds.): *Music and Copyright*, Second edition, Edinburgh: Edinburgh University Press 2004, 189-207, 192.

[21] Cf. Matthew David 2010, 32.

[22] Cf. Matthew David 2010, 33.

[23] Cf. Robert Sandall: "Off the record", in: *Prospect*, 01.08.2007, https://www.prospectmagazine.co.uk/magazine/offtherecord, accessed 06.10.2020.

[24] Robert Sandall 2007.

In 1987, the digital compression technology MP3 was developed by the German institution Fraunhofer ISS to facilitate storage and transmission of sound recordings while maintaining near-CD quality.[25] Not long after the format was patented in the US in 1996 and started to gain popularity, the music industry realized that the reproducibility of CD-Rs was the least of their problems. As they had no copy-protection system, MP3 files could be copied over and over without significant effort.[26]

When a CD is taken from someone, he looses it – but when an MP3 is transferred, both people end up with a copy and another source for sharing is created. In addition, the conversion of music from digital format to digital format resulted in no quality loss compared to analogue techniques.[27] Although there were ways to exchange audio files online before MP3 emerged (for example through WAV), these formats were very space-consuming and combined with the slow transmission speed, the download of one song often lasted hours.[28] Throughout the 1990s, computer equipment became more and more affordable and by 2000, 60 million American households had a personal computer (PC) and 43 million of them had access to the internet.[29] Since the software that was required to convert a CD into a MP3 file was freely available on the internet, 41% of all American households could now keep whole libraries of their favorite songs on their computer hard disc – ready to share. Because the MP3 format could also be used for non-infringing audio recordings, in 1998 the first tech companies announced portable MP3 players with which people could listen to "their" songs.[30] Of course, this was a thorn in the flesh of major companies, which so far relied on the consumers only having access to limited CDs, tapes and vinyls.[31] And rightly so: In 2002, the Australian economist David Throsby speculated that big record companies and music publishers could disappear completely as the internet develops.[32]

---

[25] Cf. Lee Marshall 2004, 192.

[26] Cf. Jessica Litman 2001, 154.

[27] Cf. Matthew David 2010, 32.

[28] Cf. Ariel Berschadsky: "RIAA v. Napster: A Window onto the Future of Copyright Law in the Internet Age", in: *J. Marshall J. Info. Tech. & Privacy L.*, vol. 18, no. 3 (2000), 755-790, 758-759, https://repository.jmls.edu/cgi/viewcontent.cgi?article=1190&context=jitpl, accessed 08.10.2020.

[29] Cf. Ariel Berschadsky 2000, 758.

[30] Cf. Jessica Litman 2001, 154.

[31] Radio was indeed unlimited, but consumer could not control what they heard and radio stations bought the rights for songs from the majors.

[32] Cf. David Throsby 2002, 18.

Technology reduced the labor necessary to duplicate a file to nearly zero. Matthew David, Associate Professor of Sociology at Durham University, refers to the subsequent period as "post-scarcity"[33]. He states that the physical limit of an object and the consequential "closure" of a market through scarcity is important for major companies to protect their monopoly. The rise of digital formats opens up free markets for free competition, annulling intellectual property law. This law is enforced the most by the people or companies that once benefitted from what he calls "yesterday's creative commons"[34] at some point in time. The old and established generation calls for closure and invokes property rights to ensure their position in the industry, while the newer generation demands more creative commons to promote the right to develop and creativity per se. David notices that intellectual property law on the one hand causes scarcity by regulating distribution, but on the other hand inhibits it by avoiding overuse through the "tragedy of the commons"-scenario[35]. But with an infinite resource like an MP3 file, the tragedy of the commons isn't a problem and scarcity is created for something that's infinitely available. The metaphorical saying "You can't have your cake and eat it!"[36] does not apply in the digital era. Technological innovations like file sharing are not appreciated by the established companies, but attempts are made to block them through copyright law in order to protect the monopoly, only further motivating the file sharers. As David puts it: "Intellectual property rights [...] are not natural, but constructions of interest. They express particular alliances and conflicts."[37] For a long time, copyright law effected closure to regulate the music market – but with the rise of the internet and formats like MP3, this regulation proves to be a challenge.[38]

---

[33] Matthew David 2010, 42.

[34] Matthew David 2010, 43.

[35] The tragedy of the commons refers to a situation, in which something finite is freely available. Everybody will act logically instead of collectively in order to optimize his individual benefit, what eventually results in overuse. (Cf. Margaret E. Banyan: "Tragedy of the commons", in: *Encyclopædia Britannica*, 14.05.2020, https://www.britannica.com/science/tragedy-of-the-commons, accessed 08.10.2020.).

[36] Matthew David 2010, 42.

[37] Matthew David 2010, 57.

[38] Whole paragraph: Cf. Matthew David 2010, 42-46.

3. Napster: the P2P-pioneer

In 1998, the 18 year old American computer science student Shawn Fanning developed Napster[39], a software with which the up-and-coming MP3 files could be exchanged through the internet in a quick and uncomplicated way. This first ever P2P file sharing network was inspired by the chat-system IRC, more precisely by how it exchanged information in an equal and simultaneous manner. After finishing the software in May 1999, Fanning (together with his uncle) founded the company Napster Inc. and distributed the first version to his friends and other students.[40] Even though no money was invested in advertisement, Napster started to spread like a wildfire. In October, already 4 million songs were in circulation and a few weeks after the turn of the millennium, the software reached 20 million users worldwide.[41] And the numbers kept rising: By summer of 2000, the network had around 50 to 80 million users (estimates vary)[42] and 14.000 songs were downloaded every minute[43]. According to the former audience measurement service Media Metrix, every user downloaded around 127 songs each.[44] Napster became so popular among students, that it was banned on several campuses because the high number of downloads clogged their university's network.[45]

3.1 Motivation

Thanks to the new MP3 format, storage and transmission of copied audio files was no longer a problem. The hard part was to find specific files in the depths of the web, which had to be done by combing through search engines and private links.[46] What Fanning realized is that the files were out there, but only for the people who knew how to find them.[47] With Napster, MP3s would be made available to everyone with an internet connection – no matter if "techie" or not. Fanning saw the potential of MP3 files and sought

---

[39] The name came from Fanning's nickname "Napster", which he often used in online forums.

[40] Chapter until here: Cf. Alexander Lang: *Filesharing und Strafrecht*, Berlin: Logos 2009, 31-32.

[41] Cf. Tom Lamont: "Napster: the day the music was set free", in: *The Guardian*, 24.02.2013, https://www.theguardian.com/music/2013/feb/24/napster-music-free-file-sharing, accessed 10.10.2020.

[42] Cf. Guido Brinkel: *Filesharing: Verantwortlichkeit in Peer-to-Peer-Tauschplattformen*, Tübingen: Mohr Siebeck 2006, 1.

[43] Cf. Tom Lamont 2013.

[44] Cf. Tony Smith: "Napster has huge number of users – shock!", in: *The Register*, 14.10.2000, https://www.theregister.com/2000/10/14/napster_has_huge_number/, accessed 10.10.2020.

[45] Cf. Michael Miller: *Discovering P2P*, Alameda: Sybex 2001, 120.

[46] Cf. Alexander Lang 2009, 31.

[47] Cf. Matthew David 2010, 33.

to reduce the gap between what can be done with them (regarding endless copying) and what is legal.[48]

For Jan Becker, Professor of Marketing at the KLU in Hamburg, the main reasons for the network's popularity are content, convenience and costs.[49] Every user could easily access millions of songs for free, making Napster the consumer's "holy grail" in the music industry. In addition, the network was far more reliable than insecure FTP search engines and shady "Top 100"-websites, which some people used to download MP3s prior to Napster.[50] Furthermore, a lot of people used Napster because they could acquire a specific song they liked without having to buy the whole album CD, where they paid for other multiple songs they didn't plan to listen to.[51] John Williamson, manager of the Scottish rock band Belle and Sebastian, describes Napster's business model as follows: "[Napster] had absolutely everything. [...] People love the idea of being able to find anything. You could never get access to that much stuff in any record shop."[52]

Over the years, the above-mentioned major music companies acquired dominant monopolies, making it hard for independent artists to gain ground in the industry. Since the 1980s, these independent artists, who often make music "outside the mainstream", are incorporated by the majors if they managed to build up an audience. Their sounds are then adjusted to fit the mass taste.[53] If not supported by bigger companies, the chances of these so called "indie artists/labels" (especially if they are from developing countries[54]) to benefit from the market are very small. With Napster, the first network emerged which enabled independent artists to distribute their music to millions of people without much effort. After the artists managed to build up an audience, they could sell their work the conventional way to make money. On the other hand, the amount of artists trying to promote their music rose, making the support of a major label, a commercial agent or an internet music portal beneficial.[55]

---

[48] Cf. Clay Shirky: "Listening to Napster", in: Andy Oram (ed.): *Peer-to-peer: Harnessing the benefits of a disruptive technology*, Sebastopol: O'Reilly 2001, 21-37, 28.

[49] Cf. Jan U. Becker: *File Sharing in Peer-to-Peer-Netzwerken: Ökonomische Analyse des Nutzerverhaltens*, Wiesbaden: DUV 2004, 183.

[50] Cf. Erik Möller: "Schöner tauschen", in: *Telepolis*, 30.06.2000, https://www.heise.de/tp/features/Schoener-tauschen-3450104.html, accessed 10.10.2020.

[51] Cf. Kisa West: "Napster Is Pushing Us Closer to Socialism", in: *Los Angeles Times*, 21.08.2000, https://www.latimes.com/archives/la-xpm-2000-aug-21-fi-7783-story.html, accessed 11.10.2020.

[52] Jim Rogers 2013, 59.

[53] On majors and "indies": Cf. David Throsby 2002, 10.

[54] Cf. David Throsby 2002, 18.

[55] Cf. David Throsby 2002, 13.

Another significant motivation for people to use Napster was that the established music companies didn't want to adapt to new Internet economics. They expected users to pay the same per-unit prices for an album in MP3 format than for a CD album, irrespective of the fact that these MP3 files are endlessly replicable and renewable.[56] The major companies have always kept the lion's share of sales revenue, while the artist (who is usually bound by contract) only gained a small percentage. This has been justified with the fact that what the majors do is the expensive part of the process a song goes through. With the emergence of online music market places, record pressing, CD burning and the distribution costs became optional. But still, the way the earnings were split between the company and the artist remained the same. This has motivated many music consumers to stop the financial support towards these companies and to join P2P networks, as they "don't comply because it doesn't make sense to them."[57] Some users (especially anti-globalists) considered Napster as an important step or movement towards free flow of information, what they referred to as "knowledge commons".[58] On Fanning's network, every consumer could be a publisher, and when everyone is their own publisher, everyone can be their own record company.[59] To some extend, Napster democratized the music industry by giving more power to the artist and the consumer while pushing the major companies from their dominant positions.[60] Regarding the rapid success of his network, Fanning said in 2001: "Napster works because people who love music share and participate."[61]

3.2 Structure

When the general public started to access the Internet in the 1990s, the common communication model was "client/server" based, i.e. the user initiates a temporary connection to a central well known server (for example through a web browser), downloads the content and then disconnects. This enabled the server provider to better administrate and

---

[56] Paragraph until here: Cf. Clay Shirky 2001, 34.

[57] Jessica Litman 2001, 169. On revenue distribution: Cf. Jessica Litman 2001, 168.

[58] Cf. Guido Brinkel 2006, 2. More on knowledge commons: "Commons in Action: Knowledge Commons", in: *International Association for the Study of the Commons*, 03.09.2014, https://www.youtube.com/watch?v=H3N9Gb3bKzQ, accessed 11.10.2020.

[59] Cf. Jessica Litman 2001, 155.

[60] Cf. Jim Rogers 2013, 11.

[61] Quote by Shawn Fanning: "Shawn Fanning zum Urteil gegen Napster", in: *Der Spiegel*, 13.02.2001, https://www.spiegel.de/netzwelt/tech/o-ton-shawn-fanning-zum-urteil-gegen-napster-a-117325.html, accessed 10.10.2020.

control the distribution. On Napster, every user simultaneously acted as a provider, which changed the model to "client/client", or in other words P2P.[62] When Fanning started to work on the software, he imagined a network which facilitated users to display their music collections and obtain songs from other people.[63] Since the music industry tried to take down all acts of online file sharing they could reach, a "normal" web page using the conventional model was impractical and another method had to be found.[64] Because the individual users provided the files from their own PC's disk, Napster didn't need any storage capacities in form of a central database.[65] However, Napster was not a pure P2P system. Fanning integrated a central indexing server, to which the user issues a request consisting of certain keywords describing the song he is looking to find. The indexing server then searches for peers who offer a file whose name contains the same keywords as stated in the request. If the search was successful, the indexing server returns the coordinates (usually the IP-adresses) of the peers offering the song. At last, the file exchange is made completely outside the Napster network, through a HTTP-based connection between the peers.[66]

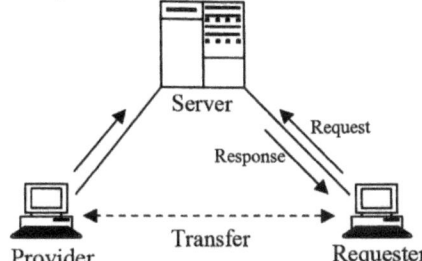

Fig. 1: How a file was acquired through Napster. (Liu/Antonopoulos 2009, 75).

This way of operation implicates that without the indexing server, file sharing through the Napster network was not possible. Napster can be described as a centralized P2P system, "facilitating sharing but also physically mediating it."[67]

---

[62] Paragraph until here: Cf. Jörg Eberspächer/Rüdiger Schollmeier: "Past and Future", in: Ralf Steinmetz/ Klaus Wehrle (eds.): *Peer-to-peer systems and applications*, Berlin et al.: Springer 2005, 17-23, 19.

[63] Cf. Matthew David 2010, 33.

[64] Cf. Clay Shirky 2001, 28.

[65] Cf. Clay Shirky 2001, 29.

[66] On Napster's indexing server: Cf. Jörg Eberspächer/Rüdiger Schollmeier: "First and Second Generation of Peer-to-Peer Systems", in: Ralf Steinmetz/Klaus Wehrle (eds.): *Peer-to-peer systems and applications*, Berlin et al.: Springer 2005, 35-56, 37.

[67] Matthew David 2010, 33.

3.3 Shutdown

In 1996, the Berne Convention underwent another revision referred to as the World Intellectual Property Organisation (WIPO) Copyright Treaty. This extension was based on Article 20 ("special agreement") of the Berne Convention and provides additional protection to authors whose works are made available on the Internet. In October of 1998, the US passed the Digital Millennium Copyright Act (DCMA) to enforce the agreements made in the WIPO Copyright Treaty concerning digital forms of infringement.[68]

When Napster started to gain popularity in early 1999, it instantly appeared on the radar of the major music companies. By December of the same year, the American record label A&M Records, 17 other labels and the Recording Industry Association of America (RIAA) filed a lawsuit against Napster Inc. at the United States District Court in San Francisco, accusing Fanning's network of facilitating copyright infringement, direct contribution to infringement and vicarious infringement as defined in the DCMA. Seven months later the district court decided that Napster had to instantly stop all copyright infringing activities being committed by it's users – but the U.S. Court of Appeals for the Ninth Circuit suspended the order two days later after Napster filed an appeal. In February 2001, the Court of Appeals confirmed the district courts decision, which found Napster Inc. guilty on all three counts, and ordered the P2P network to install a filter to prohibit copyright infringement. Napster was unable to do so and went offline in July 2001. Also, since no more income could be made through advertisement, the company wasn't able to pay the fine of US$26 million and filed for bankruptcy a year later.[69]

Napster was never accused of direct copyright infringement, but was made responsible for the actions of it's users. The court saw it as evident that the majority of songs exchanged on Napster was copyright protected by the plaintiffs and therefore shared unauthorized. By declaring the titles of the songs they are willing to share to the Napster index, the users made them publicly available, violating the "right of distribution" as defined in section 106 (3) US Copyright Law. The download of a song created a copy, which violated the "right of reproduction" as defined in section 106 (1) US Copyright Law. Napster referred to the "Fair-use-Doctrine", which is defined in section 107 US Copyright Law and can permit the use of a copyright protected song in the following

---

[68] Cf. Matthew David 2010, 34.
[69] On RIAA vs. Napster Inc. until here: Cf. Frauke Wenzl: *Musiktauschbörsen im Internet: Haftung und Rechtsschutz nach deutschem und amerikanischem Urheberrecht*, Baden-Baden: Nomos 2005, 93-94.

cases: (1) The use of a song for private and non-commercial purposes, (2) the use of a song not creative in nature, (3) the use of a small amount of a song, (4) the use of a song without negative effects on the market, (5) the use of a song for sampling[70] and (6) the download of a song for "space-shifting"[71]. But the court ruled out "fair use" as the users repetitively and exploitively downloaded complete copies of creative songs for free, achieving an enormous commercial advantage while at the same time damaging the industry.[72]

Napster Inc. argued that, just like an Internet Service Provider (ISP), it couldn't determine what files are exchanged through it's network. However, the defense was rejected as Napster's indexing server facilitated the infringement and could've been used to stop it.[73] It functioned as a central directory of all files, provided the necessary IP addresses and monitored the exchange processes, which made it evident to the court that Napster assisted the user's violations.[74]

4. P2P through the 2000s

The music industry considered Napster's shutdown a huge success, while in reality it served as a starting shot for other P2P networks to emerge. When these networks started to gain popularity in no time, it became clear that the majority of users where unimpressed by legal interferences against the providers as long as they could continue their file sharing on another platform. According to Annemarie Bridy, who is a copyright counsel at Google, there were two main reasons for why users of P2P networks wouldn't stop doing what they're doing:[75] They didn't have to and they didn't want to. They didn't have to because even after the law struck against Napster, new networks emerged and stood in for their predecessor. And they didn't want to for reasons already discussed in

---

[70] Sampling: Users only download songs for tryout, planning on buying them afterwards. It was ruled out by the court as samples are usually not complete tracks and not endlessly playable.

[71] "Space-shifting": Users only download songs in MP3 which they already bought in another format. It was ruled out by the court as it was unlikely.

[72] Whole paragraph: Cf. Frauke Wenzl 2005, 94-101.

[73] Paragraph until here: Cf. Matthew David 2010, 34.

[74] Cf. Jeff Langenderfer/Don L. Cook: "Copyright Policies and Issues Raised by A&M Records v. Napster: 'The Shot Heard 'Round the World' or 'Not with a Bang but a Whimper?'", in: *Journal of Public Policy & Marketing*, vol. 20, no. 2 (2001), 280-288, 282, https://www.jstor.org/stable/pdf/30000594.pdf?refreqid=excelsior%3A2a20271793d40ae1d6ed25e73cbc0590, accessed 14.10.2020.

[75] Cf. Annemarie Bridy: "Why Pirates (Still) Won't Behave: Regulating P2P in the Decade after Napster", in: *Rutgers Law Journal*, vol. 40, no. 3 (2009), 565-611, 600, https://osf.io/preprints/socarxiv/z57qd/, accessed 16.10.2020.

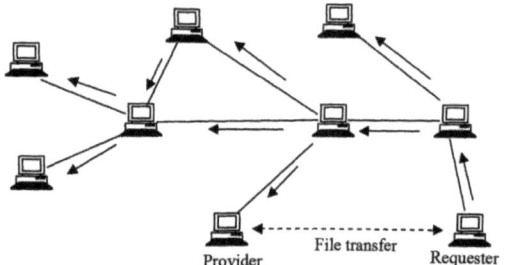

Fig. 2: How a file was acquired through Gnutella. (Liu/Antonopoulos 2009, 77).

chapter 3.1 of this paper, which according to Bridy are anchored in the "permissive social and cultural norms that have developed over the years"[76].

4.1 Decentralization

In the end, Napster's downfall was their "contributory infringement" caused by the central indexing server, which actively enabled the users to share copyright protected songs. It was originally integrated for commercial attractiveness, as a central hub that every user was passed through was appealing to advertisers.[77] Napster can be described as a centralized P2P system, in which the provider was able to monitor the user's sharing activities. The next generation of P2P networks got rid of this legal liability by creating decentralized systems, which enabled users to share files directly between each other while being completely independent of the providers.[78] A virtual network is created, which functions irrespective of the physical network and is invulnerable to restrictions from administrative authorities.[79]

One of these decentralized P2P networks is Gnutella, which first appeared in 2000 and started to gain popularity after Napster's shutdown. It is not a network by itself, but an open source software which can be used via several clients like LimeWire or Gnucleus. After the client is started, the computer looks for a certain number of neighboring "peer nodes" (peers) he can connect with. When the user then searches for a specific file, the request is transmitted to all of his neighboring nodes who check if they have it available. If so, the file transfer is made directly between the peer and the requester. If not, they forward it to their neighbors and so on. The search process continues until the file

---

[76] Annemarie Bridy 2009, 601.
[77] Cf. Matthew David 2010, 35.
[78] Cf. Matthew David 2010, 35.
[79] Cf. Jörg Eberspächer/Rüdiger Schollmeier: "Past and Future", 19.

is found or a certain time-to-live (TTL) is reached, which can be adjusted by the user and stands for the maximum amount of times a request is forwarded.[80]

This method, which is referred to as "flooding", results in a high bandwidth consumption and has therefore been modified in the newer Gnutella versions. Requests are now forwarded across "superpeers" (peers with more powerful computers), which each monitor 50 to 100 "leafnodes" (ordinary peers).[81] By doing that, these hybrid P2P networks added a hierarchical layer but at the same time kept the complete self organization and decentralization of early Gnutella. The same method was used in the P2P protocol Fast-Track, which was accessible through clients like Kazaa and Grokster.

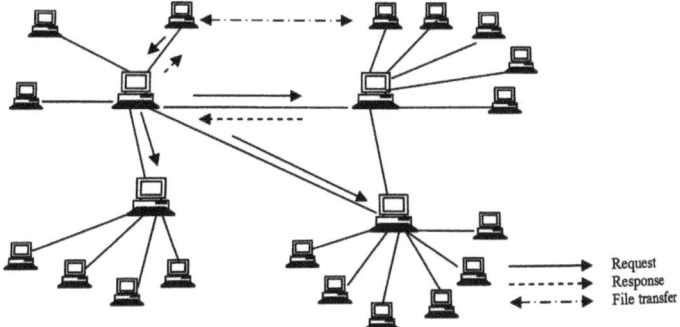

Fig. 3: How a file is acquired through FastTrack and newer Gnutella versions. (Liu/Antonopoulos 2009, 78).

In contrast to Napster (Napster Inc.), P2P networks using Gnutella or FastTrack can't be considered companies as they have no central server, no administrative control and no postal address.[82] The same goes for the P2P file sharing protocol BitTorrent, which made up 53% of all P2P traffic in June 2004. Here a file is first split up into thousands of pieces, which are then downloaded separately by different peers. Afterwards the peers exchange the missing pieces among each other and eventually all participants own a copy of the complete file.[83]

---

[80] Whole paragraph: Cf. Lu Liu/Nick Antonopoulos 2009, 76.

[81] Cf. John Buford/Heather Yu/Eng Keong Lua: *P2P Networking and Applications*, Burlington: Morgan Kaufmann 2009, 142.

[82] Cf. Gene Kan: "Gnutella", in: Detlef Schoder, Kai Fischbach, Rene Teichmann (publ.): *Peer-to-peer: ökonomische, technologische und juristische Perspektiven*, Berlin et al.: Springer 2002, 189-199, 189.

[83] On BitTorrent: Cf. Johan Pouwelse/Paweł Garbacki/Dick Epema/Henk Sips: "The Bittorrent P2P File-Sharing System: Measurements and Analysis", in: Miguel Castro/Robbert van Renesse (eds.): *Peer-to-peer systems IV: 4th International Workshop, IPTPS 2005, Ithaca, NY, USA, February 2005; revised selected papers*, Berlin et al.: Springer 2005, 205-216, 205-206.

Due to the rising number of both users and networks, the 2000s could be considered the florescence of P2P file sharing. As of June 2008, 200 million people had one or more P2P applications installed on their computer.[84]

4.2 Legal war

Just like their predecessor Napster, decentralized P2P networks were mainly used for the exchange of copyright protected works. In 2003, a lawsuit was filed at the U.S. District Court for the Central District of California against Grokster's and Morpheus's software provider, accusing him of contributory infringement and vicarious infringement. However, the court determined that the defendant had no control over what was being done with the software, couldn't interfere with the user's actions and therefore didn't contribute to infringing activities. In addition, his software could also be used for non-infringing purposes.[85] The software provider was indeed aware of the fact that some people at some time used his software for illegal actions, but there was no definite moment in which he had knowledge of an infringing activity that he could have prohibited. This verdict strengthened the confidence of other P2P software providers, as they seemed to be legally invulnerable.[86] However, 2 years later (in the case Metro-Goldwyn-Mayer Studios Inc. v. Grokster, Ltd.) the United States Supreme Court came to a different decision. The judge stated that "one who distributes a device with the object of promoting its use to infringe copyright, as shown by clear expression or other affirmative steps taken to foster infringement, is liable for the resulting acts of infringement by third parties." Grokster was convicted of inducing copyright infringement and later announced it would no longer offer it's P2P service.[87] This verdict built a foundation for the music industry on which they could legally take down P2P networks. But since most of the software was open source, new P2P networks kept emerging and the bigger pro-

---

[84] Cf. Mary Madden: "The State of Music Online: Ten Years After Napster", in: *Pew Research Center*, 15.06.2009, https://www.pewresearch.org/internet/2009/06/15/the-state-of-music-online-ten-years-after-napster/, accessed 19.10.2020.

[85] For comparison the court referred to a case from 1984 (Sony Corp. of America v. Universal City Studios, Inc). The verdict allowed Sony to continue the selling of their video recorders, which also could be used for copyright infringing actions.

[86] Paragraph until here: Cf. Frauke Wenzl 2005, 142-146.

[87] On the 2005 Grokster case: Cf. Galen Hancock: "Metro-Goldwyn-Mayer Studios Inc. v. Grokster, Ltd.: Inducing Infringement and Secondary Copyright Liability", in: *Berkeley Technology Law Journal*, vol. 21, no. 1 (2006), 189-212, 198-200, https://www.jstor.org/stable/pdf/24119545.pdf?refreqid=excelsior%3A37b38347a11bb31ad08dbd8304ddef6e, accessed 19.10.2020.

viders just moved offshore in order to take advantage of more tolerant copyright laws and weaker legal enforcement.[88] The major companies therefore started to focus on the P2P network's users whose IP addresses they were able to obtain through the ISPs. This was primarily done in the US as the EU had stricter privacy laws concerning the user's personal data.[89] By July 2006, the RIAA had initiated legal proceedings against 20,000 up-loaders and by January 2008, over 4,500 pre-litigation settlement letters had been sent to American students. The most publicized case was the one against Jammie Thomas-Rasset in 2009, who was ordered to pay the RIAA US$1.92 million for uploading 24 songs to Kazaa. The amount of lawsuits against individual file sharers started to decline as most users moved on to BitTorrent or completely scattered networks like the newer Gnutella, in which it is very hard to determine who shared what.[90]

4.3 Aftermath

The global recorded music sales (analog and digital formats combined) peaked in 1999 with a retail value of US$38.7 billion, but declined throughout the 2000s to only US$24.4 billion in 2010.[91] However, the value of "music driven" industries such as recording, live performances, publishing and others rose from US$51 billion in 1998 to over US$71 billion in 2010.[92] As to why record sales declined, it's controversial whether P2P file sharing could be considered the main cause. A study by the American economist Stan Liebowitz came to the conclusion that without P2P file sharing, there would have been a further increase in record sales from 1998 to 2003. According to his calculations, the reduction in sales due to file sharing should even be larger than the actual decline measured by the industry.[93] A 2006 study states that the downloading of music

---

[88] Cf. Seagrumn Smith: "From Napster to Kazaa: The Battle Over Peer-To-Peer Filesharing Goes International", in: *Duke Law & Technology Review*, vol. 2, no. 1 (2003), 1-9, 1, https://scholarship.law.duke.edu/cgi/viewcontent.cgi?article=1076&context=dltr, accessed 19.10.2020.

[89] Cf. Andrea Glorioso/Ugo Pagallo/Giancarlo Ruffo: "The Social Impact of P2P Systems", in: Xuemin Shen/Heather Yu/John Buford/Mursalin Akon (eds.): *Handbook of Peer-to-Peer Networking*, Berlin et al.: Springer 2009, 47-70, 52.

[90] On the RIAA's legal procedures against individual file sharers: Cf. Matthew David 2010, 62-63.

[91] Cf. Jim Rogers 2013, 32.

[92] Cf. Jim Rogers 2013, 34.

[93] Liebowitz's study: Cf. Stan J. Liebowitz: "Research Note: Testing File-Sharing's Impact on Music Album Sales in Cities", in: *Management Science*, vol. 54, no. 4 (2008), 852-859, 859, https://www.jstor.org/stable/pdf/20122431.pdf?refreqid=excelsior%3A6b06846a4124637ded326085e89af8cb, accessed 20.10.2020.

through a P2P network reduces the probability of buying music by 30%.[94] In 2007, one million people dropped out of the CD market and 48% of all American teenagers (the main audience of P2P networks) did not purchase a single CD that year.[95]

In addition, the major music companies themself denounce P2P networks as the main reason for the decline in record sales.[96] On the other hand, a 2008 study compiled for the Canadian government department Industry Canada concluded that there is no concrete evidence that P2P file sharing has a negative effect on the (Canadian) music industry. Rather it can be associated with an increase in record sales, as for every 13 song-files shared, physical sales increase by 0.44 CDs. This market creation effect can be explained with the above-mentioned sampling ("hear before buying") and with the fact that users of P2P networks are more likely to purchase music online.[97] According to a study by the music research firm The Leading Question, P2P file sharers spend four and a half times more money on digital music than people who only download from licensed sites.[98] Other reasons for the decline in record sales could be the higher availability and efficiency of CD burning technologies combined with digital media libraries, the development of portable storage devices and overall the changing consumption habits concerning the new MP3 format (e.g. only buying one track out of an album).[99] The decline in CD sales could also be explained with the fact that the major companies mostly reformatted and sold old collections and as this repertoire was exhausted, sales went down.[100] Furthermore, the industry relied too much on potential "One-Hit-Wonders", financing more and more artists which were not profitable in the long run. The companies tried to gain quick success through trendy music by targeting the audience aged 12

---

[94] Cf. Alejandro Zentner: "Measuring the Effect of File Sharing on Music Purchases", in: *The Journal of Law & Economics*, vol. 49, no. 1 (2006), 63-90, 66, https://www.jstor.org/stable/pdf/10.1086/501082.pdf?refreqid=excelsior%3A8fd9f5ee7e0bff60dacf7d25f171af27, accessed 20.10.2020.

[95] Cf. The NPD Group: „Consumers Acquired More Music in 2007, But Spent Less", in: *npd*, 26.02.2008, https://www.npd.com/press/releases/press_080226a.html, accessed 20.10.2020.

[96] Cf. Alexander Lang 2009, 41.

[97] Industry Canada study: Cf. Birgitte Andersen/Marion Frenz: "The Impact of Music Downloads and P2P File-Sharing on the Purchase of Music in Canada", in: *DIME Working Papers on Intellectual Property Rights*, no. 82 (June 2008), 1-43, 22, https://www.dime-eu.org/files/active/0/WP82-IPR.pdf, accessed 20.10.2020.

[98] Cf. Owen Gibson: "Online file sharers 'buy more music'", in: *The Guardian*, 27.07.2005, https://www.theguardian.com/technology/2005/jul/27/media.business, accessed 20.10.2020.

[99] Cf. Jim Rogers 2013, 46.

[100] Cf. Matthew David 2010, 33.

to 25, but in doing so the financially stronger older audience was neglected and revenue was missed out on.[101]

5. The new music industry

As already argued in chapter 3.1, the music industry back then failed to adapt to the new Internet economics initiated by the MP3 format, what (to some extend) induced consumers to use P2P networks. Since licensed major-label MP3 music was rarely available, P2P was the consumer's only option to get songs for his or her new portable MP3 player.[102] In order to make networks like Napster less attractive, legal alternatives with good quality and high availability had to be established. By doing that, the illegal copying of music in digital form could've been reduced to a manageable level (like it was achieved with private copying in conventional formats).[103] When the music industry adapts to the people's new expectations, for example through subscription based pricing, the "civil disobedience"[104] – and with it the use of illegal file sharing networks – will decline. The companies have to work in favor of the economic logic of the internet.[105] Also, besides from establishing new types of licensing deals for legal downloading, the industry has to rely more on on secondary income sources like merchandise and concert tours.[106] In order to stay relevant during the internet era, the major companies are forced to enter the online market – which is something they failed to do at first. They ignored the internet and tried to block all of it's advantages, instead of using it as a new revenue source.[107] The Irish composer and record producer Bill Whelan describes the industry's approach as "sluggish", arguing that the record companies weren't very creative when it comes to technological progress and it's possibilities.[108] One missed opportunity was Napster, which could've been turned into a legal download platform or a subscription based ser-

[101] On "One-Hit-Wonders" and audience targeting: Cf. Alexander Lang 2009, 42.
[102] Cf. Jessica Litman 2001, 168.
[103] Cf. David Throsby 2002, 12.
[104] Clay Shirky 2001, 35.
[105] Cf. Clay Shirky 2001, 34.
[106] Cf. Ruth Towse: "Copyright and Economics", in Simon Frith/Lee Marshall (eds.): *Music and Copyright*, Second edition, Edinburgh: Edinburgh University Press 2004, 54-69, 68.
[107] Cf. Jim Rogers 2013, 57.
[108] Cf. Jim Rogers 2013, 55-56.

vice during it's court case. If only 10% of the network's originals users would've subscribed, the revenue would've brought the industry back on track.[109]

The first step towards a "new music industry" was iTunes, which first emerged in 2003 and had a licensing agreement with all major music labels, which enabled it to offer millions of digital songs for sale. Since then, the market for digital music on the Internet has been steadily growing and global digital recorded music sales rose from US$20 million in 2002 to US$5.2 billion in 2011.[110] In 2008, iTunes was the second largest music retailer in the US after Walmart[111] and three years later, the 16 billionth song was sold[112]. With the emergence of music streaming services like the Spotify, which was released in 2008, more and more consumers acquire digital music the legal way.[113] These platforms have become a widely accepted P2P alternative for the consumer and an important sales channel for both the music companies and the artists.[114] In 2011, digital music services made up 32% of overall global revenue[115] and last year, music streaming alone accounted for 80% of the music market[116].

6. Conclusion

Intellectual property law had been working in favor of the major music companies for a long time, protecting their monopolies and regulating the market. This changed with the emergence of the MP3 format, which made a licensed song an unlimited resource on the consumer end. The first network to enable the global exchange of these MP3 files was Napster, which used a P2P architecture instead of the conventional client/server model. Apart from the fact that they were now able to access millions of songs for free, the consumers used the network because they were dissatisfied with the music industry's approach to the internet era. Due to the relatively new WIPO Copyright Treaty and the indexing server integrated into the network, Napster had to shutdown in 2001 following

---

[109] On Napster as a missed opportunity: Cf. Jim Rogers 2013, 58-59.
[110] Paragraph until here: Cf. Jim Rogers 2013, 82.
[111] Cf. The NPD Group 2008.
[112] Cf. Jim Rogers 2013, 82.
[113] Cf. Jim Rogers 2013, 89.
[114] Cf. Lauri Rechardt: "Streaming and Copyright: a Recording Industry Perspective", in: *WIPO Magazine*, May 2015, https://www.wipo.int/wipo_magazine/en/2015/02/article_0001.html, accessed 22.10.2020.
[115] Cf. Jim Rogers 2013, 82.
[116] Cf. Joshua P. Friedlander/Matthew Bass: "Mid-year 2019 RIAA Music Revenues Report", in: *RIAA*, 2019, https://www.riaa.com/wp-content/uploads/2019/09/Mid-Year-2019-RIAA-Music-Revenues-Report.pdf, accessed 22.10.2020.

a lawsuit initiated by the RIAA and multiple record labels. In the following years, several other P2P networks emerged, which were completely decentralized and therefore less susceptible to copyright law. Even though the industry had some success in taking down these advanced file sharing networks, they kept reappearing in different forms and continued to have millions of users worldwide. The music industry did experience a severe decline in revenue throughout the 2000s, but it's controversial whether P2P was solely responsible or not. Legal alternatives to P2P networks – like iTunes, 7digital and later Spotify and Deezer – could be considered the industry's knights in shining armor, as the consumers started to shift towards these platforms, leaving P2P behind. The digital world subsequently became the most profitable income source of the major music labels, for example due to Spotify, which reached 100 million paying users in 2019.[117] However, this "new music industry" is being controlled by the "big tech" companies Apple, Google and Amazon, which make it hard for new entrants to gain ground.[118] This could make one think that maybe it's time for another disruptive innovation, similar to the one P2P was. As Justin Frankel, the founder of Gnutella, once said: "I'd be giving power to people, and what can be wrong with that?"[119]

---

[117] Cf. Jon Porter: "Spotify is first to 100 million paid subscribers", in: *The Verge*, 29.04.2019, https://www.theverge.com/2019/4/29/18522297/spotify-100-million-users-apple-music-podcasting-free-users-advertising-voice-speakers, accessed 23.10.2020.
[118] Cf. Leslie M. Meier/Vincent R. Manzerolle: "Rising tides? Data capture, platform accumulation, and new monopolies in the digital music economy", in: *New Media & Society*, vol. 21, no. 3 (2019), 544-561, 555, https://journals.sagepub.com/doi/pdf/10.1177/1461444818800998, accessed 23.10.2020.
[119] David Kushner: "The World's Most Dangerous Geek", in: *davidkushner*, 13.01.2004, http://www.davidkushner.com/article/the-worlds-most-dangerous-geek/, accessed 23.10.2020.

List of references

Alejandro Zentner: "Measuring the Effect of File Sharing on Music Purchases", in: *The Journal of Law & Economics*, vol. 49, no. 1 (2006), 63-90, https://www.jstor.org/stable/pdf/10.1086/501082.pdf?refreqid=excelsior%3A8fd9f5ee7e0bff60dacf7d25f171af27, accessed 20.10.2020.

Alexander Lang: *Filesharing und Strafrecht*, Berlin: Logos 2009.

Andrea Glorioso/Ugo Pagallo/Giancarlo Ruffo: "The Social Impact of P2P Systems", in: Xuemin Shen/Heather Yu/John Buford/Mursalin Akon (eds.): *Handbook of Peer-to-Peer Networking*, Berlin et al.: Springer 2009, 47-70.

Annemarie Bridy: "Why Pirates (Still) Won't Behave: Regulating P2P in the Decade after Napster", in: *Rutgers Law Journal*, vol. 40, no. 3 (2009), 565-611, https://osf.io/preprints/socarxiv/z57qd/, accessed 16.10.2020.

Ariel Berschadsky: "RIAA v. Napster: A Window onto the Future of Copyright Law in the Internet Age", in: *J. Marshall J. Info. Tech. & Privacy L.*, vol. 18, no. 3 (2000), 755-790, https://repository.jmls.edu/cgi/viewcontent.cgi?article=1190&context=jitpl, accessed 08.10.2020.

Berit Kann: *Musikpiraterie: Ansätze zur Lösung der praktischen und juristischen Probleme unter besonderer Berücksichtigung des Urheberstrafrechts*, Münster: Lit 1995.

Birgitte Andersen/Marion Frenz: "The Impact of Music Downloads and P2P File-Sharing on the Purchase of Music in Canada", in: *DIME Working Papers on Intellectual Property Rights*, no. 82 (June 2008), 1-43, https://www.dime-eu.org/files/active/0/WP82-IPR.pdf, accessed 20.10.2020.

Clay Shirky: "Listening to Napster", in: Andy Oram (ed.): *Peer-to-peer: Harnessing the benefits of a disruptive technology*, Sebastopol: O'Reilly 2001, 21-37.

"Commons in Action: Knowledge Commons", in: *International Association for the Study of the Commons*, 03.09.2014, https://www.youtube.com/watch?v=H3N9Gb3b-KzQ, accessed 11.10.2020.

David Kushner: "The World's Most Dangerous Geek", in: *davidkushner*, 13.01.2004, http://www.davidkushner.com/article/the-worlds-most-dangerous-geek/, accessed 23.10.2020.

David Throsby: *The music industry in the new millennium: Global and local perspectives*, Paris: UNESCO Division of Arts and Cultural Enterprise 2002.

Erik Möller: "Schöner tauschen", in: *Telepolis*, 30.06.2000, https://www.heise.de/tp/features/Schoener-tauschen-3450104.html, accessed 10.10.2020.

Frauke Wenzl: *Musiktauschbörsen im Internet: Haftung und Rechtsschutz nach deutschem und amerikanischem Urheberrecht*, Baden-Baden: Nomos 2005.

Galen Hancock: "Metro-Goldwyn-Mayer Studios Inc. v. Grokster, Ltd.: Inducing In-fringement and Secondary Copyright Liability", in: *Berkeley Technology Law Journal*, vol. 21, no. 1 (2006), 189-212, https://www.jstor.org/stable/pdf/24119545.pdf? refreqid=excelsior%3A37b38347a11bb31ad08dbd8304ddef6e, accessed 19.10.2020.

Gene Kan: "Gnutella", in: Detlef Schoder, Kai Fischbach, Rene Teichmann (publ.): *Peer-to-peer: ökonomische, technologische und juristische Perspektiven*, Berlin et al.: Springer 2002, 189-199.

Gil Press: "A Very Short History Of The Internet And The Web", in: *Forbes*, 02.01.2015, https://www.forbes.com/sites/gilpress/2015/01/02/a-very-short-history-of-the-internet-and-the-web-2/#7b71b77a7a4e, accessed 01.10.2020.

Guido Brinkel: *Filesharing: Verantwortlichkeit in Peer-to-Peer-Tauschplattformen*, Tübingen: Mohr Siebeck 2006.

Jan U. Becker: *File Sharing in Peer-to-Peer-Netzwerken: Ökonomische Analyse des Nutzerverhaltens*, Wiesbaden: DUV 2004.

Jeff Langenderfer/Don L. Cook: "Copyright Policies and Issues Raised by A&M Records v. Napster: 'The Shot Heard 'Round the World' or 'Not with a Bang but a Whimper?'", in: *Journal of Public Policy & Marketing*, vol. 20, no. 2 (2001), 280-288, https://www.jstor.org/stable/pdf/30000594.pdf? refreqid=excelsior%3A2a20271793d40ae1d6ed25e73cbc0590, accessed 14.10.2020.

Jessica Litman: *Digital Copyright*, Amherst/New York: Prometheus Books 2001.

Jim Rogers: *The death and the life of the music industry in the digital age*, London: Bloomsbury 2013.

Jörg Eberspächer/Rüdiger Schollmeier: "First and Second Generation of Peer-to-Peer Systems", in: Ralf Steinmetz/Klaus Wehrle (eds.): *Peer-to-peer systems and applications*, Berlin et al.: Springer 2005, 35-56.

Jörg Eberspächer/Rüdiger Schollmeier: "Past and Future", in: Ralf Steinmetz/Klaus Wehrle (eds.): *Peer-to-peer systems and applications*, Berlin et al.: Springer 2005, 17-23.

Johan Pouwelse/Paweł Garbacki/Dick Epema/Henk Sips: "The Bittorrent P2P File-Sharing System: Measurements and Analysis", in: Miguel Castro/Robbert van Renesse (eds.): *Peer-to-peer systems IV: 4th International Workshop, IPTPS 2005, Ithaca, NY, USA, February 2005; revised selected papers*, Berlin et al.: Springer 2005, 205-216.

John Buford/Heather Yu/Eng Keong Lua: *P2P Networking and Applications*, Burlington: Morgan Kaufmann 2009.

Jon Porter: "Spotify is first to 100 million paid subscribers", in: *The Verge*, 29.04.2019, https://www.theverge.com/2019/4/29/18522297/spotify-100-million-users-apple-music-podcasting-free-users-advertising-voice-speakers, accessed 23.10.2020.

Joseph S. Dubin: "The Universal Copyright Convention", in: *California Law Review*, vol. 42, no. 1 (1954), 89-119, https://www.jstor.org/stable/pdf/3478227.pdf?refreqid=excelsior%3A2a830f3fbab813884261efb623f13405, accessed 02.10.2020.

Joshua P. Friedlander/Matthew Bass: "Mid-year 2019 RIAA Music Revenues Report", in: *RIAA*, 2019, https://www.riaa.com/wp-content/uploads/2019/09/Mid-Year-2019-RIAA-Music-Revenues-Report.pdf, accessed 22.10.2020.

Kisa West: "Napster Is Pushing Us Closer to Socialism", in: *Los Angeles Times*, 21.08.2000, https://www.latimes.com/archives/la-xpm-2000-aug-21-fi-7783-story.html, accessed 11.10.2020.

Lauri Rechardt: "Streaming and Copyright: a Recording Industry Perspective", in: *WIPO Magazine*, May 2015, https://www.wipo.int/wipo_magazine/en/2015/02/article_0001.html, accessed 22.10.2020.

Lee Marshall: "Infringers", in Simon Frith/Lee Marshall (eds.): *Music and Copyright*, Second edition, Edinburgh: Edinburgh University Press 2004, 189-207.

Leslie M. Meier/Vincent R. Manzerolle: "Rising tides? Data capture, platform accumulation, and new monopolies in the digital music economy", in: *New Media & Society*, vol. 21, no. 3 (2019), 544-561, https://journals.sagepub.com/doi/pdf/10.1177/1461444818800998, accessed 23.10.2020.

Lu Liu/Nick Antonopoulos: "From Client-Server to P2P Networking", in: Xuemin Shen/Heather Yu/John Buford/Mursalin Akon (eds.): *Handbook of Peer-to-Peer Networking*, Berlin et al.: Springer 2009, 71-89.

Margaret E. Banyan: "Tragedy of the commons", in: *Encyclopædia Britannica*, 14.05.2020, https://www.britannica.com/science/tragedy-of-the-commons, accessed 08.10.2020.

Martin Kretschmer: "Eine Lobby-Geschichte: Reflexionen zur Entwicklung des Urheberrechts", in: Lina Brion/Detlef Diederichsen (publ.): *100 Jahre Copyright*, Berlin: Matthes & Seitz, 74-99.

Martin Kretschmer/Friedemann Kawohl: "The History and Philosophy of Copyright", in Simon Frith/Lee Marshall (eds.): *Music and Copyright*, Second edition, Edinburgh: Edinburgh University Press 2004, 21-53.

Mary Madden: "The State of Music Online: Ten Years After Napster", in: *Pew Research Center*, 15.06.2009, https://www.pewresearch.org/internet/2009/06/15/the-state-of-music-online-ten-years-after-napster/, accessed 19.10.2020.

Matthew David: *Peer to Peer and the Music Industry: The Criminalization of Sharing*, Thousand Oaks: SAGE Publications 2010.

Michael Miller: *Discovering P2P*, Alameda: Sybex 2001.

Nelson Minar/Marc Hedlund: "A Network of Peers: Peer-to-Peer Models Through the History of the Internet", in: Andy Oram (ed.): *Peer-to-peer: Harnessing the benefits of a disruptive technology*, Sebastopol: O'Reilly 2001, 3-20.

Owen Gibson: "Online file sharers 'buy more music'", in: *The Guardian*, 27.07.2005, https://www.theguardian.com/technology/2005/jul/27/media.business, accessed 20.10.2020.

Robert Sandall: "Off the record", in: *Prospect*, 01.08.2007, https://www.prospectmagazine.co.uk/magazine/offtherecord, accessed 06.10.2020.

Ruth Towse: "Copyright and Economics", in Simon Frith/Lee Marshall (eds.): *Music and Copyright*, Second edition, Edinburgh: Edinburgh University Press 2004, 54-69.

Seagrumn Smith: "From Napster to Kazaa: The Battle Over Peer-To-Peer Filesharing Goes International", in: *Duke Law & Technology Review*, vol. 2, no. 1 (2003), 1-9, https://scholarship.law.duke.edu/cgi/viewcontent.cgi?article=1076&context=dltr, accessed 19.10.2020.

"Shawn Fanning zum Urteil gegen Napster", in: *Der Spiegel*, 13.02.2001, https://www.spiegel.de/netzwelt/tech/o-ton-shawn-fanning-zum-urteil-gegen-napster-a-117325.html, accessed 10.10.2020.

Stan J. Liebowitz: "Research Note: Testing File-Sharing's Impact on Music Album Sales in Cities", in: *Management Science*, vol. 54, no. 4 (2008), 852-859, https://www.jstor.org/stable/pdf/20122431.pdf?refreqid=excelsior%3A6b06846a4124637ded326085e89af8cb, accessed 20.10.2020.

The NPD Group: „Consumers Acquired More Music in 2007, But Spent Less", in: *npd*, 26.02.2008, https://www.npd.com/press/releases/press_080226a.html, accessed 20.10.2020.

Tom Lamont: "Napster: the day the music was set free", in: *The Guardian*, 24.02.2013, https://www.theguardian.com/music/2013/feb/24/napster-music-free-file-sharing, accessed 10.10.2020.

Tony Smith: "Napster has huge number of users – shock!", in: *The Register*, 14.10.2000, https://www.theregister.com/2000/10/14/napster_has_huge_number/, accessed 10.10.2020.

YOUR KNOWLEDGE HAS VALUE